# Dead Now
# Of Course

# Dead Now
# Of Course

## Phyllida Law

4th ESTATE • *London*

4th Estate
An imprint of HarperCollins *Publishers*
1 London Bridge Street
London SE1 9GF
www.4thEstate.co.uk

First published in Great Britain by 4th Estate in 2017

1 3 5 7 9 8 6 4 2

Text and illustrations copyright © Phyllida Law 2017

The right of Phyllida Law to be identified as the author
of this work has been asserted by her in accordance
with the Copyright, Design and Patents Act 1988

A catalogue record for this book is available from the British Library

ISBN 978-0-00-824474-3

Printed and bound in China

**MIX**
Paper from
responsible sources
**FSC™ C007454**

FSC™ is a non-profit international organisation established to promote
the responsible management of the world's forests. Products carrying the
FSC label are independently certified to assure consumers that they come
from forests that are managed to meet the social, economic and
ecological needs of present and future generations,
and other controlled sources.

Find out more about HarperCollins and the environment at
**www.harpercollins.co.uk/green**

*For my grandchildren,*
*Ernie, Walter, Gaia & Tindy*

'Here's tae us
Wha's like us
Damn few,
And they're a' deid'

Old Scottish toast, Anon

'Our revels now are ended. These are our actors,
As I foretold you, were all spirits, and
Are melted into air, into thin air;
And like the baseless fabric of this vision,
The cloud-capped towers, the gorgeous palaces,
The solemn temples, the great globe itself,
Yea, all which it inherit shall dissolve;
And like this insubstantial pageant faded,
Leave not a rack behind. We are such stuff
As dreams are made on, and our little life
Is rounded with a sleep.'

Prospero, *The Tempest*, Act 4, Scene 1

# OVERTURE

One September, the grown-ups started talking of this thing called War. I was evacuated from Glasgow aged seven. No one liked evacuees. They were dirty, came from Glasgow and had fleas. I was lucky: the eldest daughter in my billet was a superb storyteller. She and I improvised a mystery called 'The Red and Silver Purse', which lasted for weeks. I spent a lot of time crouched in cupboards, or underneath the gate-legged table. I think her grasp of storyline was educational.

I loved her stories, and played a lot of major characters. The War was a sideline.

———•·•———

At my school, I was the only boarder, and I loved it. The classroom window-seat was heated and the walls

were lined with books. I read all of George Eliot
– he was my favourite writer, until I found a large
medical dictionary. At thirteen, I had some very odd
symptoms and I researched them in depth. Apparently I was to die young, so I decided to devote my
life to the human race – a Scottish Mother Teresa,
with a stethoscope. I always wanted a stethoscope.

I gave up all the things I loved, like music, painting and drawing in order to pass the required exams
for the medical school in Glasgow. I got them all,
but the elderly professor, with pince-nez, said I
was too young. 'Go away,' he said. 'Go away for a
year.' I didn't have the time. In despair, I told my
mother I was to die young. She disagreed. So did
the doctor, who gave me iron pills.

The lid blew off my life. I decided to be a set
designer, without the slightest idea of how one
could achieve that ambition. I simply applied to
every drama school of which I had heard. The
Bristol Old Vic replied, asking for two speeches to
be learnt and delivered. I presented myself for the
audition in a room above a cabbage wholesaler. I'd
had the sense not to choose Juliet, and I included a

Scottish speech, from David Lyndsay's *A Satire of the Three Estates*. 'Behold my paps of pulchrytude perfyte,' I breathed. I think that was the clincher. They accepted me immediately.

My indomitable granny thought theatre the 'Gateway to Hell'. There was nothing in the family except medicine and the Church. She said she had a degree in Electricity and, of course, she knew Shakespeare. He lived on Sherbrook Avenue.

No one ever asked me for my portfolio, but I understood that the first year was to be with the actors and the second year was backstage. I had such a good time. That first year was hilarious – I didn't understand any of it. When asked to relax, I folded myself up and fell onto the floor in a heap. Each morning we did exercises in very little cloth-ing to 'The Skater's Waltz', and it was frightful. I did mine with Joe, the bridge of whose nose was rather flat because, having told his dad he wanted to be an actor, his dad thumped him. He eventually became a tax inspector.

I was trained to kiss stage left or right of the opposing mouth, leaving the face of the star contender available for the audience. When this year's young fling their clothes off and devour each other on screen, I have to leave and put the kettle on. I mean, how do they do that? What if they haven't brushed their teeth?

Romance did not flourish in Glasgow. My mother disapproved of people holding hands in the street. 'Why can't they wait till they get home?' she'd say. And eating in the street was unthinkable, as bad as smoking in the street, or wearing curlers till teatime. George Bernard Shaw thought that pushing food into a hole in the middle of one's face was revolting. He even considered that sexual activity was less offensive. At least, that's what I've heard. You may have to Google it.

Ken Tynan would certainly have preferred it. I remember catching him on TV, telling us with firm conviction that we would be seeing 'the act' on stage any day now. He was right. He actually used the word 'F***', the F word, and it was startling.

My generation was pretty hopeless. We could smoulder a bit on stage, but we were sexually timid, and a bit lumpy. Or was that just me?

My future mother-in-law burst into tears when she heard her son was to marry an actress. There's still something disturbing, I grant you, about the word 'actress'. If an MP or some other outstanding person plays fast and loose with an actress the world is unsurprised. She is certainly no better than she should be, and probably French.

# DIGS AND TOURS

Having been accepted at the Bristol Old Vic, I was told I had to look for digs. Why digs? Why are theatrical board-and-lodgings called 'digs'? It's like some archaeological event. It says in my *Chambers Dictionary*, hiding in a huge paragraph, that it is 'North American slang'. Really? It also means 'to study hard'. Quite.

I loved my first digs, when I was still a student. My landlady was tiny, gentle and profoundly deaf. She couldn't hear thunder, but if there was lightning she covered all the mirrors in the house with towels and retired to a cupboard under the stairs.

Then, on tour, there was the legendary superb cook, highly recommended by Tyrone Guthrie. Mrs Thomas was her name. She worked in a munitions factory and smuggled out sugar and scrubbing brushes. Everyone knew Mrs McKay in

Daisy Avenue, Manchester. She had two houses, one for the girls, one for the boys. She liked the boys best, and preferred them to be well known. We all swapped over one night, changing houses. She was rather upset.

We weren't allowed 'callers' either. One actor smuggled his boyfriend in by carrying him upstairs in a piggyback. 'Cripples now, Mr Cardew?' Mrs M shouted from below stairs.

We used to rehearse in the local cinema, starting at ten in the morning, when it was dim, dusty and deserted. Then we caught the bus after lunch – I don't remember lunch. The bus was a cartoon. It had about ten seats in front and the back was jammed full of our gear. There were rails for costumes and barricaded sections for the set – the flats – and a large skip for the props. The boys put up the sets, the girls ironed and sorted the costumes – sometimes we got to do a bit of nailing and I was particularly brilliant with the French brace … Don't ask.

Our gear included rugs, cushions, drinks, wellies, books, embroidery, and some of us made rag rugs. This was popular and called bodging. Sometimes we ran our lines, but we were young – we knew them.

We played everywhere possible, for miles around, even Dartmoor Prison, where I seem to remember I made my entrance ascending from a trapdoor. There were occasions when bits of the set weren't used because the set was too big for the stage. I once made an exit which I couldn't complete as the entrance was blocked by actors queuing to enter. I just had to reverse back onto the stage, trying to look intelligent and as if I were meant to be there. A door stuck once, irrevocably. They do, don't they? The actor entered through the fireplace. That was tricky.

We might have been in Sidmouth when nobody could get behind the set at all and had to exit, as one would, from the building itself. You would leave stage left, race round the library to stage right, and enter that way. If it had rained, as it often had, the effect was very comic.

It might have been the following year when we went to the Edinburgh Festival with a play about Mary, Queen of Scots by an Italian. We previewed it in a church hall, halfway up Arthur's Seat, or halfway down, depending on how you looked at it.

One famous night, we were about to give Queen Mary the last rites, when there was an ear-splitting, numbing, extended crash, as if Edinburgh Castle had collapsed and was rolling downhill in our direction. Catherine Lacey, who played Queen Mary, didn't blink. She went to her death, as ever, with great dignity.

Apparently the ceiling had collapsed in our Revue Bar, and we assumed we might have a night off. Not a bit of it. Swept clean, the joists had large bunches of chickweed stuffed into any cracks and blackened old branches were nicked from local trees and fixed to all possible corners, then hung with boots and shoes.

Brilliant. I couldn't remember what it had looked like before.

We even took the play to Linlithgow Palace, where I was very impressed by Mary, Queen

# PICCOLO
# THEATRE COMPANY

*Patrons*
Peggy Ashcroft, C.B.E.
Angela Baddeley
Glen Byam Shaw, C.B.E.
Sir Lewis Casson
George Devine
Sybil Thorndike, D.B.E.
Alec Guinness

# Mary Stuart

QUEEN OF SCOTLAND

A New Play by
## JOSEPH CHIARI

EDINBURGH FESTIVAL 1954

*Programme Threepence*

of Scots' loo. A hole in the battlements with a dizzying drop to the moat. I hope someone held onto her.

————

I don't think they do British Council Tours now like the one we did to South America. Our itinerary, gloriously, went like this: Brighton, Mexico City, Caracas, Quito, Santiago, Montevideo, Rio de Janeiro, Lisbon, Madrid, Paris, Athens and Rome. Sir Ralph Richardson, reasonably enough, wished to tour with people he liked, so he submitted a list of actors he favoured. They were all dead.

We were in Ecuador, and Patsy Byrne and I were excited, beginners, costumed and ready on stage. The band played the national anthem. It was very merry and upbeat, and Patsy and I danced to it, swirling our huge skirts as we did a very energetic jive. The assistant stage manager crept on stage and whispered that we were causing a grave diplomatic incident. In the shadow of the wings we saw stern figures glaring at us accusingly. Fortunately for us,

next up was 'God Save the Queen', so we had to dance to that too. It's not easy.

The best thing about Quito was they didn't know the plot of *The Merchant of Venice*. Imagine Sir Ralph, sharpening his knife, looking vengeful and about to cut off his pound of flesh when Barbara Jefford, as Portia, says 'Tarry a little, there is something else. This bond doth give thee here no jot of blood.' At the words 'no jot of blood', the audience stood up and cheered. Did they in Shakespeare's day, I wonder? Oh, I hope so.

When we stopped touring, I took up permanent residence in the icy attic of the local ballet school. I haven't seen hoar frost on an interior window since. We used to slither downstairs to warm up, clinging to the brass bar of the Aga cooker in the kitchen. I learnt then to love dancers for their courage and insane trust in each other. They are always injured, but they still fly on stage and die in the wings. Boys used to carry their partners aloft by the crotch. A fork-lift, really – and no sniggering.

I watched the girls darning the toes of their pointe shoes. I watched them binding their feet, covering their blisters, wiping blood from their damaged toes, and I sat at breakfast under a pulley full of jock straps and other intimate underwear. An education for a lumpen, guarded girl like me. As far as I was concerned, that kitchen was the centre of the universe. It was where the Touring Western Theatre Ballet Company was born and, besides, there were always warm leftovers in the bottom oven of the Aga. Something heavenly, like a sausage pie.

St. MARY'S HALL
NEWTON ABBOT
Tuesday, August 26th.
at 7 p.m.

WEST OF ENGLAND
BALLET COMPANY

Tickets: 1/6 ; 2/6 ; 4/-

available from :

THE LEATHER GOODS SHOP,
36, QUEEN'S ST., NEWTON ABBOT
(TELEPHONE: NEWTON ABBOT 1112)

or at the doors.

And then, of course, there were usually
two tin baths of shrouding – the cheap-
est material in the world – being
dyed some glorious colour for
costumes on the gas stove, yards of
shrouding, furnishing fabric and old
vests. Cutting and sewing occurred
upstairs in the office by the telephone,
where we kept a pile of coins to call
the police from the local phone box
when we had indecent phone calls.
They were quite frequent.

The doll we made for *Coppélia*
frequently sat at table with us. One
of the boys used to dangle her on
the end of a rope from his bedroom
in the attic so that she arrived at the
window and tapped for attention. We
were monitored by a Collie dog that
drank beer and a Siamese cat that could
open the fridge.

On one particular occasion, we forgot
to apply for the right to use a particular piece of

music. The new ballet was choreographed, complete and costumed, and we couldn't use it. We ditched the original idea and composed our own music. It was known to us then as 'Musique Concrète'. First we ran the cold tap in the bath very fiercely and recorded it backwards. Then we interfered with the rhythm, adding a few plangent notes from an empty beer bottle. It went perfectly well.

# MILDEW

The most notorious landlady in London was a Mrs Miller. For years I only knew her as a legend. She seemed always to be lunching with her bank manager – I never even had a cup of tea with mine. Norma Sheila Peta Miller was her name, NSPM – it sounded like a government department and she's now known worldwide as 'Mildew'. When I first heard of her she was landlady of a tall terraced house in Montague Street. The sort of residence Dickens would have walked past on his way to darker districts. Demolished now, of course.

I remember passing the open door of a new kitchen as this glamorous woman put the largest joint of meat I had ever seen into her oven. It was a Wednesday. She always had an 'Open Day' on Wednesday. Sitting in a high chair was a tousle-haired boy waving a tablespoon, who favoured me with a dazzling smile. He was the youngest of three sons and called Adam. The middle son, Lee, was seriously disabled in every way. When he was a baby, Mil and her lodgers used to carry him upside-down by his feet to straighten his scoliosis. Against all medical predictions, he lived till he was seventeen and would have lived longer had he not been passionate about cars. One of his similarly afflicted friends was sitting in the driving seat of a parked car and Lee put his head through the window to look at the gear lever. His friend wound the window up. The eldest son, Nick, was twenty-five when he died. Cancer. He lived until his very last ounce of time on the sofa, and his best friend set up home on the windowsill. I think he's still there.

Somehow, she knew everyone, even the Kray brothers. She said they had the cleanest fingernails she'd ever seen. Odd. I'd always heard that they cemented their enemies into those huge pillars that hold up motorways. I don't know how she knew them. I didn't ask. She also knew assorted aristocrats. I asked about that. Her husband, Able Seaman Dusty Miller, was a prisoner of war, who had escaped so regularly they'd had to put him in the worst prison to be found, and that was Colditz. And everyone in Colditz had connections at the Court. Interesting people with terrifying voices and no money. Dusty didn't have any either. By trade, he was a heating engineer and Norma Sheila Peta helped finance his workshop with her property deals. One never knew where she lived from one moment to the next, but there were always a couple of out-of-work actors living with her. The one I knew best used to do a bit of work for Dusty. When they were installing air-conditioning in a big hen-house, he dropped his spanner from a great height. The noise was so shattering that the hens fainted. Dusty didn't bear a grudge.

Her house had a shifting population, composed of actors in the attic, a couple of criminals, several dogs, an alcoholic monkey and a prostitute. They were all gay, except the prostitute, though I fancy monkeys bat both ways.

I used to call in order to visit the actors on the top floor. If N.S.P. Miller wasn't in, they threw the key down to me in an old sock. If she was in, and answered the door, she looked like Marlene Dietrich from the waist up and an unreliable charlady from the waist down, wearing socks and sordid pink mules.

I was fascinated by the stories the boys used to tell me when I called. I wanted so much to meet the monkey, which N.S.P. Miller had bought from Harrods. There used to be a zoo in Harrods. You could, apparently, order a camel and get it delivered. Mildew bought Chico because he looked so utterly miserable and took him home via the vet, where he was diagnosed with 'borderline pneumonia'. 'Give me your hand,' the vet said to Mil, and when he took it, he snipped a three-inch cuff off her cardigan and made two tiny holes at each side, thus creating a Chico-sized jumper. He survived on a regime of port and brandy. He even had his place in the local pub. In time, he became famous for his hangovers and his ability to escape to the roof. Mildew had a very close relationship with the local firemen.

Chico lived in a huge cage in the bathroom with a tiny duvet, where he used to retire, red-eyed, from the pub. His favourite friend was a mild-mannered mongrel called Mick the Greek, on which he would ride round the house, side saddle, holding onto his collar with one hand, and waving at his fans with the other.

*Chico*

Finn McCool, the Irish Wolfhound, was huge. He used to glare at people through the letterbox with his golden eyes. He was epileptic, and if he took a turn on the top landing, his descent was epic.

I never met Bitos, the Afghan hound, now known as The Flying Duster.

Just as well. He used to bite people on the nose if he smelt alcohol.

That's three dogs and a monkey, and all I had was a kitten that spent his day in the cutlery drawer.

I don't know what happened to that cast list of dogs. I do know that Chico fell in love with Mildew and became aggressive to any other males of whatever sort, belting them with poo, aimed unerringly through the bars of his cage. In the end, he went to a retirement home. For monkeys.

# STAGECRAFT

Now that I have reached old age, 'the sere, the yellow leaf' – who wrote that? I expect it was Shakespeare, it generally is. Anyway, now I have reached it I find quite disturbing a few things I used to manage without a sob.

Sitting down is one of them. What if I miss the chair and roll backwards, legs akimbo, displaying inappropriate underwear? I have to employ what used to be called 'stagecraft'. With immense physical tact I have to organize my legs to feel the edge of any seat. Quite centrally. Then it's a doddle. Lower yourself with confidence and relief. That's a touch of stagecraft, that is. It was taught in my day.

For example, you have a crowd assembled on stage for, let's say, Antony's big speech in *Julius Caesar*, and in the crowd of young actors there is one whose hand you have been directed to take.

You know the hand will be at the end of his arm, but which arm and where, in any case, will it be? Will you have to hunt in his toga?

If properly crafted the move will be easy and smooth. With his body aligned to face in the right direction, you will find his hand absolutely available.

That's stagecraft. That is what was known as stagecraft.

# GREASEPAINT

I loved it. I lived in it.

Experienced actors generally used old cigar boxes but I loved my clumsy tin-can case with two floors. The top was for greasepaint 'sticks', which always included numbers five and nine. You had to get it at the chemist, called Frizell's, on Leicester Square. Then there were slender liners, like pencils, my favourite being 'Lake', a really lowering maroon used to create wrinkles on bouncy skin. It didn't work. I looked like a tram terminus.

The bottom of my case held absolutely everything else. Mascara, paintbrushes, hairpins, nail files, nail scissors, orange sticks, toothpaste, Tampax, a corkscrew, aspirin, Polo mints, vitamin C and a little ridged bottle of J. Collis Browne's Mixture. It used to have morphine in it. A working girl's dream of bliss. Besides all this, there were the curlers, brushes, combs and two loo rolls, plus a tin of Crowes Cremine, a sort of gloop to remove make-up. It was a lot to travel with but worth it.

One fateful day I lost my tin-can case when I left my suitcase on the platform at King's Cross on my way to the Edinburgh Festival. Whoever stole it must have been alarmed by the toilet rolls.

Another thing we toured with was a bottle of 'wet white'. Very useful for ladylike arms, hands, bosoms and other such. The boys carried a bottle of 'bole', which sounded like a vocal exercise for a budding ventriloquist but, from the dictionary, I discover it is 'friable earthy clay, probably red'. Well, it was brown in our bottle and used for the chaps generally – let's say in *Julius Caesar* or *Romeo and Juliet* when the crowd had to look Italian, and as if they had seen the sun at least once.

There is an actor called Henry Mara, who always painted one arm because his chic little toga had one shoulder free and one covered. Being dyslexic he would always paint the wrong arm. All of us lived with traces of bole or wet white between our toes and in our ears.

I used quite a bit of wet white in *Ondine*. The legend in that story was that everyone would live happily in the kingdom until the servants started spouting poetry. Quite. I was the kitchen maid. In other words – I was Death. So I was a bit pale. My costume was designed by a Greek and was original to say the least. Entering covered with yards of muslin, I looked like a portaloo. On arrival at my designated spot, I pulled two strings and was revealed in a purple nightie and a floor-length black wig made from yak's hair. Thankfully I can't remember the poem.

Moira Shearer played Ondine and needed no wet white. She was transparent already.

Peter O'Toole played three parts in *Ondine*: Superintendent of the Theatre, First Fisherman and Executioner. I saw none of them as I struggled with wet white and yards of yak hair.

I must have had expert help to go blue. When we did *A Midsummer Night's Dream* all the fairies went blue. Except Puck. He refused. As Titania, I also lit up. My headdress was covered with lights worked by a battery that I hid down the back of my bustier.

Inevitably over the weeks my bustier stretched, the batteries fell out and the lights started to flash, as they do beside a traffic accident. I only knew because the fairies became unmanageable.

False eyelashes were rather expensive so I made mine. I used to ram two hatpins into my desk, six inches apart. Then I would tie two to three strands of black Sylko between them both.

You must first find a good head of hair. Dark and strong. There was a chap who fitted the bill

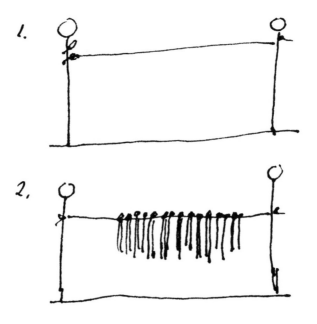

perfectly. I harvested his hair for a season. Cut to convenient lengths, I would blanket-stitch his hairs over the Sylko creating a deep fringe.

When I'd made a decent length I wrapped a knitting needle in loo roll, wrapped the strands round the same and covered them with another layer of hair, leaving them overnight. Next day, unwrapped, they were well curled. I would trim them to length and width, then stick them to my eyelids with Johnson & Johnson eyelash glue from the USA.

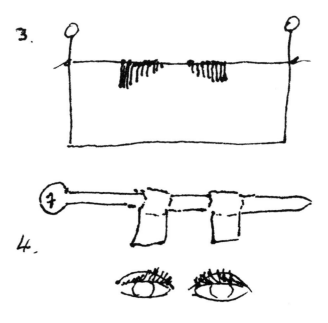

A good layer of mascara and that's the job done.

A good layer of mascara, however, requires your small box with its brush and a fine supply of spit. Spit has the perfect consistency for sticking to a lash.

I had my mascara analyzed once and it was full of my last sandwich.

Perhaps at this point, and emboldened by spit, I should mention 'moustache bleach'.

Once, years later when Ted Heath was rationing electricity and we were *all* at certain points in the dark, I picked up a medicine bottle which I confidently assumed was cough mixture and swigged bleach. It was horrific.

I had to eat two whole raw eggs.

---

'Hot Black' sounds like a jazz quartet, but it is, or was, an extreme and balletic form of mascara. It came in a block, of course, and I would scrape bits off into a teaspoon. An old teaspoon. I heated it over a candle flame and when it was molten and glutinous, I used it to create a blob at the end of each lash. It takes care and skill, using a pin or a cocktail stick. Great for some period pieces and especially for pantomime.

Hot Black

But I wouldn't try it at home. Health and Safety would never allow it, these days, but what do they know?

I may even bomb them when I'm Queen.

Nowadays, of course, you can buy astonishing lashes, sequined and curled beyond my old efforts. It's a shame.

I'm told that some people made their lashes with paper. They drew a tiny toothbrush, snipped it into lashes and stuck them on with Johnson & Johnson eyelash glue. Just don't cry. Not immediately anyway.

Another oddity was the red dot at the corner of the eye.

I still don't know what it's for but Barbra Streisand used it. Heaven knows what that red dot did to her. I have a feeling it died with footlights.

Talking of noses, I used to make mine with Plasticine, but nowadays they make them with mortician's wax. When you have modelled your nose, leave the mould to harden. Especially if it's Plasticine. Then cover with a fine layer of Vaseline. Then paint a thin layer of Copydex all over the surface and leave it to dry, warts and all. When it's dry, repeat. Three goes should be adequate. Peel off the mould very gently and you will have a perfect lightweight false nose, which can be glued in place with Copydex, which only smells for a bit.

# FOOTLIGHTS

Footlights: they've gone. I don't know where. I don't know why. I always thought that the glow they gave got rid of double chins, warmed the face and added sparkle to exhausted eyes. They had their problems, which included a tendency to explode and frighten the front row.

Once when we were in deepest Devon playing in a tiny town hall, someone was caught short. The loo was a complex journey involving collisions with the audience, so we peed in an old paint can behind the backcloth. An actor who shall be nameless tripped over it in the dark and a gently persistent trickle of pee moved inexorably downstage. I watched transfixed as it struck the first footlight and fused the set with a triumphant shriek.

On another occasion I was playing Mother Bundle in *Sleeping Beauty*, she being the wicked fairy who had a forbidden spinning wheel in the attic. I sat knitting all the wool off my spinning wheel, drank Gordon's gin from the bottle and had a large ear trumpet, which got blocked by a mouse that I ate (just a sugar one, which I dropped into my mouth by its string tail, making the audience squeal in horror). When the crew heard I had a serious hangover they filled my prop gin bottle with the real stuff. At the first sip I had the same reaction as I'd had for moustache bleach. I spat it out in a fine spray, which hit the footlights. They exploded. Of course they did. There was quite a lot of smoke.

(I expect I finished off footlights.)

# RUDE BITS

People wouldn't blink at the word 'arse', these days. But in the 1950s we weren't even allowed to use 'fart'. And, depending on who said it, 'bum' was a bit dodgy. One director tapped me on mine and said, 'You could play anything you wanted, if you could just get rid of your bottom,' whereupon the movement master suggested I went to a gynae-cologist. He was Austrian so had difficulty saying it.

I was rather humiliated.

But I'm all right now. You can say what you like to me.

At the Windmill Theatre, the girls were naked, but they were not allowed to move.

Nudity was a rare experience.

My auntie Urelda fancied a lovely actor called Gerald Harper, who was in a TV series, and when she discovered I knew him, she begged me, on her behalf, to stop him ever taking his clothes off. 'Every scrap of respect is lost,' she said.

I can't remember if I complied.

When Miles Malleson came to do *The Prodigious Snob*, a French farce, four of us girls were cast to be dancers. 'What are we to wear?' we asked anxiously.

'Absolutely nothing whatever,' Mr Malleson said.

We were in shock for a week, until he relented. Personally as bald as a coot, he wore, daily, a very effective toupee, but on stage, he would put a bald wig on top of the toupee for the play.

# PROPS!

I love Props. By which I mean the team known as
Props, because they deal with that department. If
you need anything, just call for Props. They're the
chaps who always know where the loos are, and
their skill is legendary. If a scene requires you to
take tea, Props are tucked around the set, ready
with Thermos and kettle, so that the steam is consis-
tent and so is the tea. Drinks are very demanding.
Look at Pacino in *Scent of a Woman*. He makes a
massive speech sitting with a tumbler of whisky. If
he takes a swallow, the level in the glass has to be
corrected for any retake, or each time the dialogue
is resumed. (Not easy to fiddle with such a prop in
the middle of an aria by a star.) I remember notic-
ing the whisky level moving up and down in that
speech and thought anxiously about Props. It's the
same with necklaces, scarves, chains and other such

adornments, but that's Wardrobe. One gets used to a gentle hand interfering with one's costume for one reason or another.

Quick Change

Props cook, of course. A *bête noire* of mine is eating. Glorious dinner parties are just ignored, and if an actor takes a bite, he doesn't seem to chew and he never seems to swallow. It drives me mad, but then he might choke.

We used to create easily heatable meals on tour in the West Country. We always travelled with gravy browning for whisky, tea and sherry, bolstered with cochineal for wine and port. Mashed potato was essential, and as a colleague once said to me, 'If you don't have a banana, you're fucked.'

Harold Innocent was once described to me as 'the best sitting-down actor in Britain'. We were in a TV drama together. Harold was dolled up in pink satin breeches because it was an eighteenth-century thing – I can't remember what it was. Anyway, he was standing by the monitor, chatting and smoking, when his cue came to appear. He stuffed his fags and a box of matches into the leg of his breeks, no pockets, you see. He had to play an emotional scene, which included falling on his knees before some woman. He did so rather violently and burst into flames. Props rushed on, biffed him about and took him off to inspect the damage. It was considerable. He had to go to a wee Glasgow doctor's and sit in a waiting room for ages, smelling of smoke and singed flesh, dressed in pink satin breeches.

Everyone smoked a lot in those days. Look at old films: everyone smokes and everyone drinks. Props again.

I've never smoked. I tried when I was about eight. My cousin Eleanor and I researched the whole business in the loo and, thank heaven, decided against it. It made our eyes water. I've never managed the cigarette ballet: I only managed to bend fags and on stage I became embarrassing. I'm told I used to accept a light to start smoking, and in some inadvertent way I put out the proffered light with a violent breeze from my nostrils. I couldn't inhale or breathe smoke down my nose, timed to a cue. It's a remarkable talent.

Pubs were painful places so, sadly, I missed beer. There was wine, Blue Nun and Nicolas in a box with a tap, but I don't think we could afford wine until we were over thirty. I've made up for that since.

# OPEN-PLAN THEATRES

Sitting the other night in the audience of one of our distinguished 'open-plan' theatres, I heard a confidently patrician voice declare, 'I'm so over the proscenium arch, aren't you?'

Well, no.

I miss it.

Often.

Backstage, I miss that careful announcement, 'Curtain up.' I miss it for the weight of the folds, the way its velvet moves from dark to glowing warmth, the way it starts the music. I don't mind watching the stagehands moving props while I'm having my ice cream, but in open-plan theatre, audience members park their handbags and even their feet on what I consider to be sacred ground.

It stops my breath. I can't bear it.

# WIGS AND
# WARDROBE

My mother used to say, when the mists in Argyll came down round her ears, 'It's as grey as a plumber's wig.' It is, in fact, 'grey as a plover's wing', but I prefer her version. Wigs used to be called 'rugs', but now I hear they're called 'transformations', or is that just for toupees? And why 'toupee'? It sounds like an Indian tent.

I still have my old wooden wig block, but usually they're canvas and possible for pins. We used to dress our wigs every night for something like, say, *The Rivals*. Ringlets were renewed, with rag curlers, waves pinched, clamped and sprayed generously. On Saturday night they went back to Wig Creations and were returned in perfect condition for the Monday-night performance.

Talking of hairspray, there was a gorgeous actor called Peter Wyngarde, who was famous for his dark curls, flared trousers, silk cravats and elegant cigarette holders. One night on stage he was smoking his cigarette in such an ostentatiously balletic manner that his hair caught fire. A fellow actor rushed over, took his hair off and stamped on it. No one had known he wore a toupee. This event was not widely publicized.

I watched *Four Weddings and a Funeral* last night – goodness knows how many times I've watched it. That wonderful Welsh actor Kenneth Griffith in a tiny part was really the best thing in it. He was always richly original. Once I played Titania to his Oberon, and during a break in his performance, he called on the fairies in Dressing Room 10, where he was having a mild flirtation with Mustard-seed. Tardy with his call for Act Two, he rushed on stage, swirling his vast net cloak and ignoring rather puzzled, intermittent gusts of laughter from the audience. His cloak was liberally decorated with a large pink bra and other inappropriate underwear. He'd swept them up on his way through the dressing room.

———

Robert Helpmann was an experience. He always looked alarmingly elegant. Every item of his clothing was monogrammed, down to his velvet pumps.

He was epic on stage.

There's a story that Noël Coward came backstage to see him and, met at the stage door by the stage director, he said, 'That backcloth, who slept in it last night?' Obviously it was frightfully crumpled.

'That's not the backcloth,' said the stage director. 'That's Robert Helpmann's cloak.'

That's true.

We were used to working with shrouding at 1/6d per yard, so I was particularly fascinated by dancers wearing elasticated material. There were several of them on stage, and it looked like a wind farm. Dancers got off stage by creeping into tunnels that looked like packets of Toblerone. Martha Graham was elasticated. Somebody asked

Wind Farm.

Helpmann how he'd enjoyed it. 'Very much,' he said. 'She reminded me of our dog Daisy who went blind and bumped into furniture.'

If it got boring, we moved the furniture. The design was probably a bit pallid for a star who was known to wear rings on his toes.

Bling on a big toe? Surely that's painful.

———————

I read somewhere that Orson Welles, aged nineteen or so, was playing a minor role at the Gate Theatre in Dublin when Micheál Mac Liammóir got *all* the light. He was spot-lit, and Welles was in the shade, so he spent that night sewing sequins all over his costume.

I once saw Micheál Mac Liammóir doing a one-man show. The gossip then was that he'd had very early facelifts and they kept slipping. His hair was dyed as black as Martha Graham's. Not helpful to either of them.

I think it unwise to dye your hair black.

———————

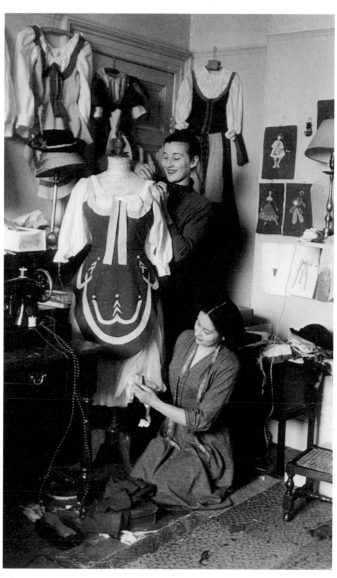

Wardrobe Assistant?

Design disaster?

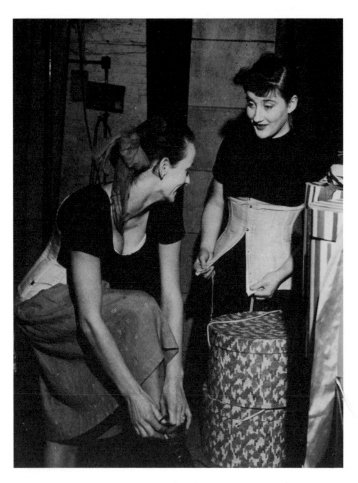

Playtex living girdle?

I did odd jobs in Wardrobe, which in Bristol was on the same level as the fly gallery. I loved that space, high up, dusty, dark and mysterious. The boys in the fly gallery looked as though they'd been born up there. They emerged from the gloom like apparitions. They loved period costumes with corsets – 'You've got lovely little milkers, pet,' they'd say. (When you're an assistant stage manager or on your first job, you'd be asked to bring the stage manager the 'key of the grid'. There is no such thing. There is no key, there is no grid.) If you were a lead, or just a lovely person, your hem would be hand-stitched. If you were rude or rubbish, your hem was machined. I was put on hooks and eyes, and I was hopeless at it. I'm telling you, it's tricky.

# CURTAIN CALLS
# AND ENTRANCES

I take a forensic interest in curtain calls. I can't approve of an exhausted actor acting 'exhausted', but he certainly can't skip on as though he's off to the Groucho Club for a drink with Ophelia. It's a delicate balance. On some shows I take pleasure in noting who is under-dressed for the curtain call. Socks are a giveaway. Now and again some character seems to be offering another a lift home as they wander into the wings chatting. If it's a musical, the orchestra often has a blissful hover-craft effect on the audience as they rise from their seats. The best curtain call I've ever seen was after a play with the Lunts, Alfred and Lynn. A final curtain went up, catching the Lunts walking off into the wings, holding hands. They were delight-fully embarrassed and enchanted to be bowing yet again. The audience loved it. Their applause had a special crescendo and was spiked with laughter. We all loved the Lunts. What we weren't told was that they did that every night.

One of my fondest theatrical memories is of a visit to London from Glasgow with my brother to see Danny Kaye, who was, as they say, huge at the time.

We sat in high excitement as the heavy swag curtains twitched and lifted. But it was to an entirely deserted stage. Not a prop in sight. I'd never seen such a thing before.

A silent stage.

No one there.

The orchestra tailed off miserably and the silence darkened. Gradually the audience became restless.

Then, quite suddenly, Danny Kaye flew from the wings, as if he'd been pushed.

He *had* been pushed.

Finally, he sat down with his legs dangling into the orchestra pit and asked for a cup of tea.

He got one.

Best opening sequence I ever saw.

# OFF

That wonderful actor Wilfrid Lawson, dead now, of course, went to a performance of *Peer Gynt* at the Old Vic, which had had wonderful reviews. After the interval, as he settled into his seat, he said to his neighbour, 'This is the best bit. This is where I come on.' He must have been rather shocked to see his understudy.

He was, as they say in the trade, 'off'.

Newton Blick sounds like a station, but was in fact a gift to the theatre, a lovely actor. He was sitting in warm sunshine one afternoon, watching the audience pouring out of the front of the Vaudeville. He was warm, relaxed and happy, till he realized they were the audience of a matinee performance in which he should have appeared.

He, too, was 'off'.

One actor I knew was picking apples in the country when his cue came up. That was tricky.

I've been an understudy myself, of course. The frock never quite fits. Nowadays I think (probably at the National) everything's digitized. In my day it was just an exercise book with a pencil attached by a string.

# NAME-DROPPING

I suppose I must have been six or seven when I ran through the foyer of my uncle's flat in London and went lickety-split into a pair of grey flannels. Someone in the sky (God?) said, 'Oops-a-daisy.'

Picked up and steadied on my patent leather pumps, I dealt with my socks and went to find my mother. She was standing stock still by the lift, eyes lowered as if she was in church.

'Do you know who that was?' she asked, in a tiny voice.

'He had a green hat,' I said.

'It was John Gielgud. I saw him playing Richard II only last week.' I wondered what had happened to Richard the First.

I didn't bump into many people quite like that. I did once follow Graham Greene from Piccadilly to the Ritz. He went in. I went home.

And I once stood in a queue behind Alastair Sim.

———•———

Alec Guinness liked the odd visit to his dressing room, to say hello, of an evening. Just to catch up on everything. One night, calling before the half, I found him in his towelling dressing-gown, socks and slippers, smoking a cigar and talking on the phone.

'That's wonderful news, Ralph,' he said, as he waved me to stay. 'Give her our love, do, I'm so glad you rang. It's wonderful news. I'll spread it. Brilliant. Brilliant. Thank you for ringing, Ralph. Wonderful news.' He put the phone down.

It was his wife, Lady Mu, who had been very seriously ill with a hysterectomy. The priest had come round to give her the last rites. She told him to 'Fuck off.'

Years later we were all playing in John Mortimer's *A Voyage Round My Father* when Alec went to Fortnum & Mason to buy his matinee tea, smoked salmon on brown.

The gentleman who served him said, 'Hello, sir. Haven't seen you for years. What are you doing these days?'

And Alec said, 'I'm at the Haymarket.'

And the chap said, 'Oh, very good. My brother has a fish stall there.'

They used to bring tea to the audience in the matinee interval at the Haymarket. A proper tea, on a tray, proper teapots, jugs, little bowls of lump sugar and a slab of very black fruit cake. It was served by harassed wee ladies in Lyons Corner House outfits, with those things on their heads that made them look quite unhinged. When the interval ended, the curtain would rise, and the first few minutes of the second half would be accompanied by the clatter of china and cutlery as anxious little ladies would try to get your tray from the middle of the row. Insane, really.

———•—•———

Paul Copley was well into his nineties when he took over a significant role in *Richard II*. On his opening night, standing in the wings, shoulder to shoulder with another actor and waiting for their cue, Paul said to him quietly, 'What's my first line?'

I remember a very famous elderly actor, Esmond Knight, who'd been almost blinded on the bridge of the *Hood* during the war. He didn't let it bother him. He used to mark the stage out with yellow gaffer tape so he knew which way he had to advance into the set, and the edge of the scenery was heavily marked, so he didn't tumble into the orchestra pit. He didn't care: he was wonderful.

———·——

Listening to the radio one afternoon, there was a sudden and unexpected blast of the Warsaw Concerto, bringing to mind that gorgeous creature Anton Walbrook, sitting at the piano, pretending to play and reducing me to rubble. I saw him once in a play at the King's Theatre in Glasgow. When he entered through double doors, centre stage, there was a surge of applause from the audience. He paused, impassive, and then bowed, minimally, as 'twere to the Queen. Then he moved quietly across the stage, to where his leading actress – who was it I wonder? I can't remember – lay seductively on an impressive double bed. Without change of expression and in the same rhythm, Anton Walbrook gently picked up a satin fold of her nightie and placed it across her breast, which had slipped out by mistake. Nothing anyone said after that had much effect.

———•———

We were rehearsing for *Noises Off* at the Savoy, and having a morning cuppa in the Props Department, when Bobby Flemyng arrived a little late, a little out of breath, wearing an old Puffa jacket and a new black eye. 'Altercation on the tube,' he said. He must have been seventy. Standing at the door of a crammed carriage he had seen, looking down, his watch lying on the floor. One of those silver engineering jobs, like a suspension bridge, that blokes buy for a lot of money on aeroplanes. He'd bent to pick it up and met another hand, doing the same thing. 'That's mine,' both hands shouted. Doors opening, they fell onto the platform, pushing and biffing each other about, and the police were called.

We were very impressed.

Bobby, realizing he would be late for rehearsal, chose a moment when the police and his assailant were surrounded by witnesses and escaped niftily up a convenient escalator.

Reaching safety, he looked at his left wrist only to discover his watch had never left it.

———·——

Michael Gambon, during a run of *Uncle Vanya* in the West End, got a bit bored, so when he went on stage he whispered to the nearest actor, 'Do you smell smoke?' The actor sniffed and passed on the query. Soon the entire stage was manned by actors sniffing and looking increasingly worried. Good fun.

That's enough name-dropping for the moment.

# NORMAN POPHAM

The most loyal and persistent theatrical fan I ever knew who came to every play, especially in Bristol where he lived, was Norman Popham. He served in a fish shop at the top of Park Road just opposite Bristol University. He wore a black leather apron, heavy wooden-soled clogs and tortoiseshell bottle-bottom specs.

Each time he came he would bring to the stage door a bunch of flowers for the prettiest girl in the production.

I never got one.

He must have saved every penny he earned because he travelled quite a lot. On one visit to Paris and the Comédie Française, the leading actress was so taken with him that she drove him to Le Bourget for his flight home. He even went to the theatre in what was, in those days, Yugoslavia, where they were so surprised to find he was a fish-monger that they interviewed him on TV. They assumed that only the aristocracy went to the theatre in England. So there was Norman Popham in his flat cap talking about Shakespeare in his perfect Bristolian accent. I was always Phyllidal. A banana was always a bananal. I suppose Yugoslavia was Yugoslavial.

Well, then they honoured him with an invitation to their production of *King Lear*.

'How was it?' we asked, over the haddock.

'There was an awful lot of blood,' he said.

When his mother became frail he used to bring bunches of flowers she had made with crêpe paper. 'Gives her something to do,' he said.

He used to bring his bouquets to London theatres and I saw him once at the stage door of the Garrick before he disappeared.

It must have been a good decade later when I was leaving the theatre for home after a performance of *Noises Off* – we were at the Savoy at the time. I passed the beautiful Gabrielle Drake's dressing room, and there I saw a stalwart bespectacled

*68*

individual in an amazing amount of leather: cap, coat, briefcase and shoulder bag.

'*Norman Popham!*' I yelled, 'I haven't seen you for years. Where have you been?'

'Moscow,' he said. 'I am married, Phyllidal, to a most wonderful woman. My mother-in-law is an angel. I have a little lad, I work in a library now and we live in the most beautiful place in the world.'

'Where?' I managed.

'Siberial,' he said.

# DRESSING ROOM
# NUMBER 10

The cast of Dressing Room Number 10 at the London Old Vic was on the top floor of the house and we were known as:

| | |
|---|---|
| *Filthy* | Me |
| *Smelly* | Andrée Melly |
| *Grimy* | Barbara Grimes |

Dressing Room Number 11, opposite, had a shifting population of chaps who got a quid more than we did. Typical. I have to admit, though, that some of them had named parts and one or two actually said things. Out loud. In blank verse.

Number 10 was our home, really. My actual digs in Chelsea are now a 'garden centre'. Then they were twenty-five shillings per week, which was nothing out of my weekly pay. I loved my little room. It had a gas fire, two gas brackets and a single gas ring. I kept a milk saucepan, a tin of Horlicks, a box of cereal and some milk on top of my wardrobe. I never washed the saucepan. I just let it grow a skin. The bath was in the kitchen and it was sometimes occupied. My landlady was appalled. Being so proper, she always wore a hat.

To get to Chelsea after the show I often walked across Waterloo Bridge to catch the number 11 bus on the Strand. My mother didn't like the sound of that. Years later, of course, there were people on Waterloo Bridge with poisonous umbrellas and she'd say to me, 'One man has been taken to hospital. Don't talk to any Russians.' But I loved that walk. It's poetry still.

One particular night, however, I took a bus across the bridge because I'd had a severe beating from an osteopath and wasn't up to the walk. I'd pulled a muscle in my groin trying and failing to do the splits, besides which my high-kicks were a bit low. Both talents were required for a French farce called *The Italian Straw Hat*, which we'd been playing for quite a while.

Sitting on the bus, I could revel in the view, because the Houses of Parliament were lit up. 'They must be sitting,' someone said. Well, it was nearly midnight.

Next day in *The Times*, it was reported that Sir Somebody had kept them all up late at night to complain that the National Theatre of England – a.k.a. the Old Vic – was showing 'some foreign rubbish', which included 'indecent dancing'. The can-can? I was thrilled – especially as I'd met the MP and knew he was to be avoided.

———————

Sometimes we fell victim to what were called 'pea-soupers'. Fog. Dense fog. It was spectacular. West End theatres closed because the audience couldn't see the stage. We couldn't see from one wing to the other. Actors just disappeared and materialized. The smell was noxious. I used to wear

a damp nylon stocking over my nose and mouth, a bit like you see them do now in Beijing.

Unable to get to Chelsea, I stayed with an aunt and walked to Hyde Park through a Victorian London. Bus conductors, those much-missed people, carried a torch and walked alongside their bus, lighting the kerb for the bemused driver. My chest coped, but it made me sick. The silence was spooky. People died. Birds left London.

I don't think Edinburgh gets fog. It's a very windy city.

# DRESSING
# ROOM 11

Dressing Room 10 and Dressing Room 11 went
with *Romeo and Juliet* to the Edinburgh Festival.
It must have been in the early 1950s. We played at
the Assembly Rooms, where we were required to
rush up and down a vomitorium. There were two.
I wonder what the plural is – vomitoria, vomito-
rios, vomitorii? Sounds disgusting anyway. I looked
up 'vomitorium' in my *Collins Dictionary* and
found a long paragraph concerned with stomach
complaints, including yellow and black vomit, in
which there was a short sentence about a door, and
I quote, 'allows a crowd to exit'. Nothing about
entering, which the boys did in some number.
Dipping his spear to clear the door and raising it to
process down the 'vom', one of the chaps arrived
on stage with a ladies' hat on the end of his spear.

Andrée Melly (a.k.a. Smelly), dressed as a nun, carrying a large battery-operated candle, took a wrong turning in the Stygian dark and ended up whizzing round the audience, like a firefly on speed.

We were always sleepless in Edinburgh. The large pilastered slate clock on the mantelpiece of our shared bedroom used to clear its throat ostentatiously, then strike every hour. It took two of us to carry it into the corridor.

———·——

Back in London we were on call for *The Merchant of Venice*. Two masked ladies were required for the court scene. We were to be dressed in yards of rustling taffeta, three-cornered hats and gold Venetian half-masks. Since there were three of us, and you couldn't see who was who underneath a Venetian fancy dress, we took turns to have a night off.

No one noticed.

I would take a late train to Bristol and spend the night in the Old Vic's paint dock where I was

*Venetian Fancy Dress*

working on the sets for a production of *Peter and the Wolf.* I used to sneak a couple of hours' sleep on stage in a huge double bed that composed most of the set of their production of *Volpone.* Late one night I was dozing gently when I felt the bedding sliding off my shoulders. Opening one eye, I saw a huge rat climbing up my blanket. I caught up with sleep on the train back.

# THEATRE ROYAL

KING STREET, BRISTOL
Founded 1766

# THE MERCHANT OF VENICE

by
WILLIAM SHAKESPEARE

THE
## BRISTOL OLD VIC COMPANY

presented by

THE OLD VIC TRUST LTD.

in association with

THE ARTS COUNCIL
OF GREAT BRITAIN

Programme 6d.

Tuesday, March 1st 1955.                    For FOUR Weeks.

# THE
# MERCHANT OF VENICE
## By WILLIAM SHAKESPEARE

The cast in the order of their appearance:

ANTONIO (a merchant of Venice) ... MICHAEL ALLINSON
SOLANIO ⎱ (friends of              ........ PETER NICHOLS
SALERIO ⎰ Antonio and Bassanio) ........ RONALD HINES
BASSANIO (suitor to Portia) .............. JOHN HUMPHRY
LORENZO (in love with Jessica) ... EDWARD HARDWICKE
GRATIANO (a friend of Antonio) ........... JOHN CAIRNEY
PORTIA (a rich heiress) ................. ROSEMARY HARRIS
NERISSA (her gentlewoman) ........... PERLITA NEILSON
BALTHASAR ⎱ (Servants to Portia) ···· GEOFFREY WRIGHT
STEPHANO ⎰                    ...... TOM KNEEBONE
LADY-IN-WAITING to Portia .............. GILLIAN LEWIS
SHYLOCK (a rich Jew) .................... EDGAR WREFORD
THE PRINCE OF MOROCCO (suitor to Portia)
                                        PETER WYLDE
LAUNCELOT GOBBO (servant to Shylock) BRUCE SHARMAN
OLD GOBBO (his father) ................. ANTONY TUCKEY
LEONARDO ⎱ (Servants to Bassanio)  GRAHAM CURNOW
GUITARIST ⎰                    ...... BRYAN DALY
JESSICA (daughter to Shylock) .............. PHYLLIDA LAW
THE PRINCE OF ARRAGON (suitor to Portia) ... PAUL LEE
SERVANT to Antonio .................... BRUCE SHARMAN
TUBAL (a Jew, of Shylock's tribe) ...... ANTONY TUCKEY
THE DUKE OF VENICE ........................... PAUL LEE
GAOLER ....................................... PETER WYLDE


Produced by JOHN MOODY

Settings designed by PATRICK ROBERTSON

If it had been Sir Ralph Richardson or his wife Lady Meriel they would have taken it home with them. Sir Ralph kept a rat called Lord North, which used to perch on his chest and delicately take sugar from his moustache. They loved rats, the Richardsons, and mice. On tour in Lisbon I found a tiny Portuguese mouse skipping about in Lady Mu's bouquet, from the night before – an extra afternoon performance had been slotted in that day. When I told Lady Mu about her mouse, she insisted I told Sir Ralph. I was very shy, but I just about managed to spit it out. He took it very seriously, swinging round from his make-up mirror to look at me steadily. 'No one told it there was a matinee,' he said. Apparently, mice are skilled timekeepers.

———————

A theatre must be a perfect place for a rat. All those pipes, all those ropes, all those crumbs that audiences leave behind in all the dark corners. One lady rat raised a large family in one of Wendy Hiller's hats. She had tucked it on top of her wardrobe in her dressing room as an understudy hat. She was probably playing Lady Bracknell.

———

One young actor I knew got a bit fed up with the rather intrusive shopping habits of a resident rat, which laid out his titbits in a line, for ease of transport to his lair. A bed became available elsewhere in Chorlton-cum-Hardy so he packed up and moved in immediately. Next day he found a familiar line of food, reaching from table to wainscot. The rat had travelled with him in his skip. One of those big basketwork theatre skips. Lovely.

———

Playing near a hotel restaurant, there was, of course, a lot of interest. Mainly from cockroaches. Some of them looked like Volkswagen Beetles that moved at thirty miles an hour. A lovely actor called Glyn Grain had to lie still, flat on the floor of the stage, in *Noises Off* (just by the Savoy

Hotel), which of course was of immense interest to any passing beetle. He was always bald with terror, unable to move.

Obviously a problem could be the theatre cat, but he has to be secured at curtain up in case he waltzes onto the stage when Hamlet is dying.

Well, it has been known.

Next came Robert Donat from his latest film to play Thomas Becket in T. S. Eliot's *Murder in the Cathedral*.

Dressing Room 10 was in the chorus. The ladies' chorus. Which went vocally from very young to ancient. I was very young and I was stationed on the top step of a flight of stairs coming from the orchestra pit. I was dressed in a lot of blankets and balancing a stone pot. Donat entered from the pit just close by. He had a dangerously bronchitic chest, which I could hear rattling with his every breath as he awaited his cue. He added to the rattle with Fox's Glacier Mint wrappers and distilled water. Then he appeared. Very slowly. And the audience erupted with wild applause. People in the gods shouted, 'Welcome home.'

I think he bowed.

We wept.

The only line I can remember saying was 'Does the bird sing in the south?'

One of the other girls had to say, 'We have to keep our households in order.'

Robert Helpmann, who was directing, came on stage and took her into the wings. She came back looking rather pink. He had told her to enunciate very clearly. What he had heard was 'We have to keep our arseholes in order.'

# THE OLD VIC THEATRE

Waterloo Road, S.E.1

Licensed by the Lord Chamberlain to GEORGE CHAMBERLAIN

The Old Vic Trust Ltd.

presents

# THE OLD VIC COMPANY

6<sup>D</sup>

in

# MURDER IN THE CATHEDRAL

T. S. Eliot

Director of The Old Vic :          Administrative Director :
   HUGH HUNT                          ALFRED FRANCIS

The Old Vic works by arrangement with the Joint Council of the National Theatre and the
Old Vic, and in full association with the Arts Council of Great Britain

# Murder in the Cathedral

*by*

### T. S. ELIOT

| | |
|---|---|
| Archbishop Thomas Becket | ... ROBERT DONAT |
| 1st Priest | ALAN DOBIE |
| 2nd Priest | WOLFE MORRIS |
| 3rd Priest | PATRICK WYMARK |
| Messenger | BRUCE SHARMAN |
| 1st Tempter | .. JOHN WARNER |
| 2nd Tempter | DOUGLAS CAMPBELL |
| 3rd Tempter | NEWTON BLICK |
| 4th Tempter | WILLIAM SQUIRE |
| 1st Knight | .. PAUL ROGERS |
| 2nd Knight | ROBIN BAILEY |
| 3rd Knight | .. DANIEL THORNDIKE |
| 4th Knight | JOHN PHILLIPS |
| Monks | PETER AUGUSTINE |
| | BERNARD KILBY |
| | DENIS RAYMOND |
| | ERIC THOMPSON |

Women of Canterbury :

| | |
|---|---|
| YVONNE COULETTE | JOSÉE RICHARD |
| BARBARA GRIMES | PHYLLIDA LAW |
| ANDREE MELLY | SONIA GRAHAM |
| JANET JOYE | CAROLINE KEITH |
| JUDITH NELMES | IRENE SUTCLIFFE |
| JENNIFER WALLACE | DORIT WELLES |

| | | |
|---|---|---|
| Choir | LUCAS BASSETT | DESMOND CAMPBELL |
| | ROBERT DAVIES | J. R. EVANS |
| | ROLAND LUCANTONIO | DAVID SARON |
| | DAVID SHARPE | JEREMY WILKIN |

Produced by ROBERT HELPMANN

Sets and costumes by ALAN BARLOW

4

# TYRONE
# GUTHRIE

Us kids from D10 and D11 adored him. I'm sure we had more fun than the principals. Someone told us that they had lent Guthrie a book, I can't remember what it was called, and it was faithfully returned, with a fried egg between its pages.

I used to take paper and a pencil to rehearsal, in case I forgot his notes.

On one occasion, in some processional scene, he clapped his hands, snapped his fingers and said to us, 'I want it to look like a rice pudding boiling.' Lovely.

There was in fact a huge procession planned in his production of *Henry VIII*.

Guthrie cast the youngest actors for the oldest parts and they had a ball. Can you imagine the make-up?

There was one scene I watched every night. Newton Blick and James Ottaway came onto the empty stage, carrying a picnic and a map. They sat on the edge of the stage, legs dangling into the pit. Little legs in wrinkled tights. They brought the procession to life, as they pretended to watch it passing at the back of the stalls. It was my favourite scene in the play, composed of two lines:

Jimmy Ottaway: 'Is that the Duke of Norfolk?'

Newtie Blick: 'Yes.'

And then, in the presence's chamber, the cardinal had called for the women to appear. When he saw Anne Boleyn and Henry, Guthrie said, 'I want to hear fly buttons hitting the ceiling.'

Us girls from D10 attended Queen Katherine with our tapestry work. Props asked Guthrie for measurements of the basket of wool. He gave it his considered opinion, and when the basket arrived, it would have fitted a small horse, or Queen Katherine herself.

She was being played by a distinguished actress, Gwen Ffrangcon-Davies, who rehearsed in a felt hat. (All the principal ladies rehearsed in hats.)

She would sit there, being Queen, tears streaming down her cheeks. And then she would make her exit and thump the banister rail to get herself an extra round of applause.

There was a gala performance of *Henry VIII*. The audience wore all its family jewels. Tiaras winked and flashed all over the stalls. The Duchess of Argyll was blinding, and Churchill was in the front row, reading the script and having difficulty with cuts and rearrangements. He was noisily confused.

———•—•———

Poking about in the rubbish at the back of my brain, I find Tyrone Guthrie in black tie giving a lecture on casting: 'You start at the very top of the profession and you end up with the telephone book.'

I wonder if he acted when he was young. I've always preferred a director who's worked at the coal face.

## The
# OLD VIC THEATRE
### Waterloo Road S.E.1.

*In the presence of*

## Her Majesty the Queen

*and*

*In Honour of the Coronation*

*a*

## Gala Performance

*of*

*Shakespeare's*

## King Henry VIII

*Wednesday 6th May 1953*

# KING HENRY VIII

## WILLIAM SHAKESPEARE

*Characters in order of speaking :*

| | |
|---|---|
| Prologue .. .. .. .. .. .. | WYNNE CLARK |
| Duke of Buckingham .. .. .. .. | LEO GENN |
| Duke of Norfolk .. .. .. .. | .. JOHN PHILLIPS |
| Lord Abergavenny .. .. .. .. | .. ERIC THOMPSON |
| Duke of Suffolk .. .. .. .. | PATRICK WYMARK |
| Cardinal Wolsey .. .. .. .. | ALEXANDER KNOX |
| Gardiner, *Bishop of Winchester* .. .. | LAURENCE HARDY |
| Brandon .. .. .. .. .. | DAVID WALLER |
| Sergeant .. .. .. .. .. | GARTH ADAMS |
| King Henry VIII .. .. .. .. | PAUL ROGERS |
| Queen Katharine .. .. .. | GWEN FFRANGCON-DAVIES |
| Surveyor to the Duke of Buckingham .. | .. WOLFE MORRIS |
| Lord Chamberlain .. .. .. .. | ROBERT HARDY |
| Lord Sands .. .. .. .. .. | JAMES OTTAWAY |
| Sir Thomas Lovell .. .. .. .. | .. ALAN DOBIE |
| Sir Henry Guildford .. .. .. | BERNARD KILBY |
| Anne Bullen .. .. .. .. .. | JEANETTE STERKE |
| A Gentleman .. .. .. .. .. | .. NEWTON BLICK |
| Cardinal Campeius .. .. .. .. | .. JOHN WARNER |
| Old Lady, *friend to Anne Bullen* .. .. | .. WYNNE CLARK |
| Bishop of Lincoln .. .. .. .. | BRUCE SHARMAN |
| Griffiths, *Gentleman Usher to Queen Katharine* | .. WOLFE MORRIS |
| Earl of Surrey .. .. .. .. | .. DANIEL THORNDIKE |
| Cromwell, *Servant to Wolsey* .. .. | TIMOTHY BATESON |
| Patience, *Woman to Queen Katharine* | MARGARET COURTENAY |
| A Messenger .. .. .. .. .. | NORMAN FRASER |
| Capucius, *Ambassador from the Emperor Charles V* | |
| | DENIS RAYMOND |
| Page .. .. .. .. .. .. | .. TERRY WALE |
| Cranmer, *Archbishop of Canterbury* .. | WILLIAM SQUIRE |
| Porter .. .. .. .. .. .. | NEWTON BLICK |
| Porter's Man .. .. .. .. | .. JOHN WARNER |

Nobles, Bishops, Clerks, Masquers, Men at Arms, Ladies :

| | |
|---|---|
| GARTH ADAMS | WILLIAM JOB |
| DAVID BENSON | FLETCHER LIGHTFOOT |
| MALCOLM BLACK | GERALD LIMBRICK |
| FRED BRAUN | JOHAN MALHERBE |
| DON BURGESS | LESLIE PITT |
| HOWELL DAVIES | DESMOND RAYNER |
| DENZIL ELLIS | ELSA BACH |
| NORMAN FRASER | SONIA GRAHAM |
| PHILIP GALE | BARBARA GRIMES |
| RUPERT HARVEY | PHYLLIDA LAW |
| PAT HORGAN | BARBARA ST. LEDGER |

Choir :

| | |
|---|---|
| ALBERT BARKER | ROLAND LUCANTONIO |
| LUCAS BASSETT | MICHAEL O'FARRELL |
| DESMOND CAMPBELL | BRIAN MATTHEWS |
| FELIX DABROWA | DAVID SARON |
| ROBERT DAVIES | DAVID SHARPE |
| J. R. EVANS | JEREMY WILKIN |

# DIRECTORS

I've only actively disliked one director. He shall remain nameless. Because I've forgotten his name. We were all working on an Irish Season at the Mermaid in London. We worked very hard, playing at night and coming in the next morning for rehearsal at ten sharp. And this particular director, ignoring all of our hard graft, would come in, turn his chair away from us, so that we just saw his back, then have a little table set beside him. Props would bring him a big mug of hot, sweet tea, which he drank while he was reading the script, and we were behind him. We couldn't see anything, and we certainly didn't have any tea. How rude.

Noël Coward requested that his cast should come to the first rehearsal word perfect. I can't approve. I learnt my lines with a sort of Pelmanism. If you're on the right-hand side of the stage,

stage right, near a sofa, that's when you say, 'The phone's ringing' or 'She's leaving you.'

Then there are directors who know all about iambic pentameter. They've probably been to Oxford or Cambridge, perhaps both.

Listen, Shakespeare never went to either.

Then you have directors who give you line readings, which is very difficult indeed because you're trapped in somebody else's thought.

One of my least favourite things are run-throughs at the end of a rehearsal period and it all gets very serious. The auditorium is dark, the director is sitting in there with his notes and you're on stage, giving what you hope to be a brilliant performance. A light in the stalls goes on. It's the torch the director is holding. It goes on because he's writing something awful about your performance. I don't think they put the light on to write, 'That was very brilliant.'

# EXTRA JOBS

One or two of our mates were in rep, earning their living in Nottingham, or Chorlton-cum-Hardy, and two DELs (Dressing Room 11s) were porters at Euston. They had a cap, an armband and a helpful income from tips. They were particularly good at getting taxis. Such a useful talent.

One impressive young man lived off a van of damp matches. He would sell to one store, and when he got a furious complaint about the quality of the goods, he apologized profusely and bought them back at once, admittedly at a slightly lower price but that, of course, was accepted. He sold them again to someone else and repeated the procedure, making a profit each time.

Peter O'Toole apparently sold yo-yos outside Selfridges.

I was deeply immersed in backstage biz at the Bristol Old Vic, making props. I seem to think that I was decorating a little oil lamp – so it must have been *Aladdin* by V. C. Clinton-Baddeley? (I'd always wondered what the V. C. stood for but his name in full was apparently Victor Vaughan Reynolds Geraint Clinton Clinton-Baddeley!) – when someone wandered in and said there'd been a phone call enquiring for me. 'ME? REALLY? WHO?'

'Len at Stage Door will know.'

He didn't.

'It sounded like a man, wanted to know if you were available.'

Oooh.

'He didn't leave a number, but he'll ring again.'

And he did.

'Can you get to Exmouth by tomorrow?' he said. 'We're doing *Hindle Wakes*. Get a copy of the Samuel French edition. It's "Ma", she's in her sixties, but you'll be perfect.'

I must have been all of twenty-two.

I got to Exmouth by teatime the next day, and one of the chaps from Dressing Room 11, the one with strong black hair, useful for eyelashes, met every train from Bristol and took me to my digs. Our landlady, Mrs Francis, was rather nice. She used to wear the same blue tweed suit every day with baggy box pleats, old brogues, wrinkled tan tights and a neat bun. I can't forget her awful spaghetti milk pudding, which I hid in my chest of drawers till her dog discovered it, so then I put it down the loo.

Talking of which, d'you remember that unforgiving loo paper? Izal, it was called.

Not fit for purpose.

# THE RUSSIANS

I had the particular advantage of having a contract as assistant stage manager in the main house at the Bristol Old Vic, with special dispensation to assist in scene painting and wardrobe. That may have been how I managed to be in Covent Garden when the Russians were ironing their tutus. Large, serious, silent women: two touring steam irons. They had jugs of water by their ironing boards. They would take a mouthful and, with spectacular control, spray it from their lips in a very fine, almost invisible cloud of droplets. Don't try this at home. I did. I just dribbled.

To see the Russians was our ambition. To meet them was a dream. A lovely actor called Graham Crowden used to queue at the stage door of Sadler's Wells, I think it was, in an attempt to get them to come to tea. They went about in pairs and looked hunted. Well, they were.

I was very disillusioned about Stanislavsky at this point because in his book, portentously named *My Life In Art*, he says that 'To play an Englishman you just dry your top teeth thoroughly and stick your top lip to the result.' It works for about a minute and makes you sound like Terry-Thomas. What's more, I found an old sepia photograph of him, reading with his cast in his study, and he is the only person there with a glass of … is it water? Could it be vodka? Tea? And it's covered carefully with a piece of card. Nobody else has anything. As I said before, I think that's rude. But I loved the fact that he'd cast a real *baboushka* to walk across the stage in a crowd scene. She was so remarkable he had to 'let her go'. She made the actors look ridiculous.

Despite my rather rancid attitude, I was still utterly determined to get a ticket for *Uncle Vanya*. A couple of the boys from Dressing Room 11 queued from first thing in the morning, and my mate, the front half of Daisy the Cow, seemed to be there all night. When reinforcements arrived, she went to the pub

Daisy

with the ticket touts. She was a dancer and went en pointe. The back end, known as 'the udder half', was me. I did a bit of tap and a little soft-shoe shuffle in my wellies. We were a triumph. Over the run, we had to invent a contract. No pulses, no garlic, no onions.

Every busker in London knew about that queue – we even had Wilson, Keppel & Betty. I considered staying out there. I loved music hall.

*Uncle Vanya* was not music hall. There was very little humour, and Vanya shouted quite a surprising amount. But I still remember the opening sequence. It was the poetry of the everyday, and I was a child looking through a window at a different world.

As for the Bolshoi, what I remember most clearly were the costumed stage management, who looked like the KGB in hats and wrinkly tights, like my landlady in Exmouth. One of them simply stared at the audience and grinned as he moved the scenery. Then there was a lovely moment when a prop tree suddenly and nervously appeared halfway up the proscenium arch. Clinging to an unconvincing black branch was a terrified ballerina, who nearly fell into the orchestra pit.

# TOM

It must have been when my brother James had his motor accident that Cupid lit a very long fuse. The news came when I was playing Julia in *The Rivals* at Bristol. There was no way I could leave to see James in hospital and there were no details about his injuries, except that they were serious. Life-threatening, I think they call it, don't they? Mother was in Glasgow getting dire, inaccurate details on the phone. Everyone else was somewhere else. Even though I hadn't seen him for months, it was Tom I thought of immediately. I rang him. It wasn't a long call: he didn't need any details. He just went. He was the mate who had met every train to Exmouth from Bristol (the one with strong black hair, useful for eyelashes) when I was to join the company. Even now I remember working in Chorlton-cum-Hardy when an actress fainted in her dressing room. Tom, alerted, asked for a window to be opened and just picked her up in his arms and carried her there. I found myself wishing it was me.

I knew he watched me if I played the piano and we'd had a snog in the back seat of the touring bus, but I was twenty-three and most of the time rather taken with an Older Man. It's a phase.

Then there was his jacket. He always wore an old corduroy jacket, pin-cord it was called, and it had aged beautifully. I always said the jacket was the clincher. A comfort blanket. If I took his arm and he was wearing the jacket, I felt at home. He was rather like a wild animal who has eyes at the side of its head – you don't know what it's thinking. He didn't smile much because his front teeth had been chipped in a cricket match, and he never made a ha-ha laugh: he wheezed. It was my ambition to make him wheeze.

We found ourselves together again in the panto-mime at Bristol. We had the Christmas party at the ballet school, and on Boxing Night I was clearing up the detritus of a wild evening in the dance studio when I found a figure crouching in the half-light from a large Christmas tree decorated with candles and Tampax. Tom. He was staring at the floor with an empty glass in his hand. As I took it from him, he said, 'Will you marry me, Philly?'

Well, I thought he was drunk.

We remained strangely silent, those last few days of the year. I heard him telling someone that we were, apparently, not talking to each other. He didn't look at me much. He wasn't sulking, just didn't look at me much. It was dismal. And New Year's Eve can be rather challenging in circumstances like that, can't it? I was snivelling in my dressing room and washing my feet in the basin. It's difficult. Good balance is required, and weeping is not recommended.

What is it about these strong, silent types? They occupy their own climate. Children are drawn in. Soon a pudgy little hand will quietly tap on an available knee. Conversation is slow to begin. But it is top secret.

I've seen this happen about once in the theatre. I was sitting in the back stalls of a play, and when the curtain went up on the first act, there was a distinguished gentleman sitting at a writing desk.

Writing, and thinking, and writing, and thinking. The audience were completely still and fascinated. I wanted to get up and walk down the aisle to the orchestra pit and see what he was writing, how it was affecting him, everything about him. It went on for absolutely ages.

Some people can create that atmosphere by themselves. Fascinating. Mr Thompson did. I wouldn't have been surprised to see him doing the *Times* crossword with a baby on his lap. Any old baby. Or to have seen him playing bridge and the baby smoking Gauloises, with a mug of PG Tips, very strong, two sugars, please.

'Ask him,' I said to Fred, the assistant stage manager, 'if he'll ask the question again.'

Fred came back rather swiftly and said, 'He said, "What question?"'

I went dripping out of my dressing room and found him. 'You asked me to marry you. Can you ask again?'

He didn't answer. He walked calmly down the stairs to the orchestra pit. Then there was a huge eruption from the drumming department.

I scrubbed my face with a hankie and went to watch from the stage. He saw me. He really saw me. It was the sort of look one would share when one was arriving at a station or an airport, having been away from home for far too long. Or it might have been the look on the orchestral conductor's face when you get your harmony right for the first time. I was always terrible at harmony, though on that occasion I don't think I was. I asked Tom for a dance. He was a terrible dancer. I had hoped he would waltz me into the wings for a proper proposal. But somebody had got there first. Tom, dressed as a pirate, went to tidy up the drum kit. I was still in a turban and a clattering concoction of fake jewellery – so it must have been *Aladdin*. I was trying to improve my looks when someone in the corridor shouted, 'A phone's free,' and I hurtled down to the booth, rang the Old Vic and spoke to the stage-door man there. 'Ernie, can you tell Bunny I rang to wish him a happy new year?'

'He skipped the curtain call, darling,' Ernie said. 'He's on the train to Bristol.' It happens in dreams, doesn't it? People move around as usual, but the sound goes.

Bunny.

Bunny. I've forgotten Bunny.

Hell in a bucket. I forgot Bunny.

He was my older man, with a gentle Canadian accent and had the best conversational Donald Duck I ever heard. Irresistible. Plus, he wore a bomber jacket and denim and he smoked Passing Clouds. Born in East London, he was inspired by a film about the Royal Canadian Mounted Police, in their scarlet jackets and wide-brimmed hats so he ran away to join them. He failed his riding test, so he ended up in the theatre, at Stratford, Ontario, and he wanted me to go back there with him.

I didn't want to go.

And they didn't want me.

Instead of a honeymoon evening, it was an emotional disaster. Bunny and I spent most of the night on a damp bench, so miserable we didn't speak. I mean, what can you say? Our domestic castle had collapsed, leaving us clinging to the scaffolding.

Bunny went back to a happy ending in Canada and, after a few painful weeks, Tom appeared at my dressing-room door to say simply, 'The cast list is up.' It was for *A Midsummer Night's Dream*. I was to play Titania, Tom was to play Puck. Thus we were thrown together again and, this time, took root.

We moved into a condemned house, in a condemned attic, up a condemned staircase, with not even a banister rail. Tom banged nails into things, I made gingham curtains – I think there might even have been a geranium in a pot. Very *La Bohème*.

We used the loo downstairs because there was a note pinned to ours: 'No Solids From This Facility Please'.

I took to cooking. My first effort was a Queen of Puddings, which went so wrong that I hid it in a wardrobe and made another.

Tom took to cooking. He stuffed a mackerel with gooseberries and stitched it up with pink thread.

His last effort was a dish called Huntington Fidget Pie. It was rather good, actually. His signature dish was Fried Cheese: strong Cheddar, grated onto a tin plate and put on the gas. Absolutely delicious.

He washed up too.

I don't remember that he had many irritating habits. The worst was that he wouldn't pass on messages. If anyone left a message on the telephone, he would always say, 'Of course I'll pass it on. Thanks very much. Bye.' I never heard a word. Men. They're all like that, aren't they?

His golfing gear was simply hideous. He had a terrible terracotta towelling top with a white zip. Frightful. And then the worst, I think, was when he ate ripe pears. He made the most disgusting squelchy noises. But you don't get many ripe pears, do you?

The most remarkable thing about him, things about him, were his eyes. Two of them. They were huge and black. If you tripped up, you'd slip over the edge and never be seen again. An American colleague passed him in a rehearsal and said, 'His eyes are very far apart. Can he see?' Fortunately, his younger child has inherited them. His eyes. Both of them.

We didn't shout much, I don't think. But we did throw things. Tom once asked what my interests were. I threw a meringue at him.

So, I never had a proper proposal of marriage. We just evolved. We didn't kiss in the street, we never held hands in the street. My mother would have so approved. But our roots were six years deep. In fact, we were doing rather well without grown-ups, and now there were three car-loads coming in our direction.

One particular Saturday, I was carefully applying my blue body paint when Tom put his head round the door. 'Call from your mother. Can we get married on May the twenty-fifth?'

I don't remember saying anything. I might have said, 'What?' or even 'Why?' but certainly, 'It's a matinee day.'

'They've planned it to the last detail,' he said. 'It's a killer. There will be three car-loads and we're

TOM.

19 Nov 1957

ROYAL

# THEATRE ROYAL

KING STREET, BRISTOL

Founded 1766

# A MIDSUMMER NIGHT'S DREAM

by

WILLIAM SHAKESPEARE

THE

## BRISTOL OLD VIC COMPANY

presented by

THE OLD VIC TRUST LTD.

in association with

THE ARTS COUNCIL

OF GREAT BRITAIN

Programme 6d.

# A MIDSUMMER NIGHT'S DREAM

## By WILLIAM SHAKESPEARE

Characters in order of their appearance:

THESEUS, Duke of Athens ...................... DAVID KELLY
HIPPOLYTA, Queen of the Amazons ......... SHEILA ALLEN
PHILOSTRATE ..................... MICHAEL DONALDSON
EGEUS, Father to Hermia ........................ JACK ALLEN
HERMIA ............................. WENDY HUTCHINSON
DEMETRIUS ................................. JOHN WOODVINE
LYSANDER ................................... PETER O'TOOLE
HELENA ................................ WENDY WILLIAMS
QUINCE, a carpenter .............. EDWARD HARDWICKE
BOTTOM, a weaver ........................ JOSEPH O'CONOR
FLUTE, a bellows-mender .................. BRUCE SHARMAN
STARVELING, a tailor ..................... BARRY WILSHER
SNOUT, a tinker ................................ ROBERT LANG
SNUG, a joiner ...................................... JOHN FLOYD
PUCK ...................................... ERIC THOMPSON
PEASEBLOSSOM .......................... VALERIE GEARON
OBERON, King of the Fairies ............... COLIN JEAVONS
TITANIA, Queen of the Fairies ............ PHYLLIDA LAW
COBWEB ...................................... ADRIENNE HILL
MOTH ............................................... JILL DALTRY
MUSTARDSEED ............................. HAZEL WRIGHT

Produced by JOHN MOODY

Settings by PATRICK ROBERTSON
Costumes by ROSEMARY VERCOE

Music specially composed by KENNETH MOBBS
Dances arranged by RAFAEL SHELLY

all to meet in Bath at the Hole in the Wall. Then we have to check them into the Suspension Bridge Hotel, because they're coming to *The Dream* in the evening, with supper afterwards at Bernie's steak house.' I felt as if I'd been run over.

Had we not been playing that night I think I would have run away. Tom would have found me sooner or later and then we could have put a girdle round the Earth in forty minutes. He came into my room a little further this time, gloriously costumed in nothing much to speak of. 'We have two whole weeks,' he said.

'People will think we're pregnant,' I said.

He came in a little further and very gently stroked a strand of my hair from my forehead. 'Let's walk home tonight,' he said. And we did. When we got home I was wearing my cardigan upside down.

Then a few evenings later, around the half-hour, Tom came into my dressing room, looking young and worried. 'We can't possibly get married in that register office,' he said. 'There's a HUGE notice, ordering us Not to Spit on the Stairs.'

As it so happened, I was able to say, 'I've just had a telegram from my ma. It says, "Prefer marriage in a church". It means we have to audition a church.' We did.

# THE WEDDING

Something old, something new, something borrowed and something blue.

Old? Tom? And then a new wedding ring, of course, was out of the question: they were eight guineas – more than a week's wages. So we went to the Christmas Steps and bought a beautiful rose-gold keeper ring, delicately engraved, and it was only thirty-five shillings. The lady behind the counter who served us said, 'Shall I wrap it, or will you wear it now?' It's still on – look.

Something new was my dress. I bought it in Country Casuals on Park Street in Bristol. It was made of oyster pink grosgrain and fitted me no-where. Absolutely nowhere. The less said the better. I have photos.

Borrowed. Something borrowed. I borrowed Ma's little marcasite earrings, but I have them still so that's wrong. Then, during the service, I wept sweet tears and Tom quietly handed me a perfectly laundered white hankie from the top pocket of his suit.

Blue. Something blue. Then I remembered that I was blue. I'd been blue for weeks as Titania – I spent quite a lot of my married life blue because little scraps of it hung behind my ears and round my toes. As I say, it lasted well into my married life.

With the church we had found lovely Canon Gaye, neat and merry in his leather-belted frock, offering us lunch after the ceremony, should we need it, before the performance, and he gave a poetic dissertation on marriage that I barely heard as my nose was running. 'The habit of love,' he said, 'takes root, enriches your life and the lives of those around you.'

That lovely actor Jack Allen turned to his neighbour, tears streaming down his cheeks, and said, 'He's *so* wrong.'

My mother, enchanted, blew a kiss to Canon Gaye across the nave – he said it was a first.

We did it!

I came to in the vestry, where you go to sign the register. I felt at home in the vestry. You get a kiss in the vestry.

Sealed with a kiss.

Chaste and gentle.

I stopped shivering and the world took a deep breath.

# FINALE

The following Sunday, we took the train to London to look for work. 'Did you cash that cheque?' I asked.

'What cheque?'

I'd had a cheque for thirty quid from a set design I had made for Darlington Hall. I meant it to go to Hungary – it was 1956. I had to concede that the cash would be needed for digs and unforeseen dramatic consequences, so I shut up.

Tom said, 'We need it for London,' and he patted his pockets, like men do – that quasi-religious ritual of spectacles, testicles, watch and wallet. Otherwise, all he seemed to have were his fags, the *Times* crossword and a fishing rod. I had a sewing-machine, and the Agony Corner, which I'd packed the week before, plus: earplugs, Dr Collis Browne's Mixture, Senokot, Askit powders,

aspirin, Germolene, herbal calming pills, Gold Spot
for bad breath and a packet of wine gums.

A cab at Euston was easy: two guys from Dressing Room 11 were on the platform in peaked caps,
acting 'being porters'. They whisked us to the rank
and fixed a large notice 'Just Married' to the taxi's
bumpers, plus several tin cans. We got them off by
Marble Arch.

I had thought we were on the way to our favourite greasy spoon to eat, but Mr Thompson had
booked a bed for the night upstairs in an old-fashioned restaurant that had been patronized by
my aunts throughout the war. I never knew there
were beds involved.

In the morning Tom bought the *Evening Standard* and *The Times*, and I bought *The Lady* and
*The Stage*.

We saw some frightful places. One had a large
gas stove in a small stair cupboard. Under the stairs,
indeed. In the end, we found 25 Royal Crescent.

There was a small kitchen, but if you wanted to
have a bath, you had to attach a hose to the kitchen

The Royal Borough of Kensington

ROYAL
CRESCENT, W.11

hot tap and place the hose carefully over a small, very ineffectual wall, and fill the bath like that.

I don't remember having a bath.

We were always out of work.

Mr Thompson very often wrote a short story for the BBC. It was fifteen quid. Saved our lives.

The first story, I remember, was about the deeds for Piccadilly Circus. Someone wanted to build something posh there, and found out that Piccadilly Circus was owned, from way back, by this elderly lady.

Good idea.

Then Tom got a job at Sadler's Wells with a friend, moving the scenery, from opera to opera.

And so we began.

Mr and Mrs Thompson. Mr and Mrs Eric Thompson.

I had a husband. He had a wife.

Ridiculous.

# PHOTOGRAPHS
# AND PROGRAMMES